ADAM HAMILTON

Author of *Creed: What Christians Believe and Why*

THE
WALK

FIVE ESSENTIAL PRACTICES
OF THE CHRISTIAN LIFE

YOUTH STUDY BOOK

By Josh Tinley

Abingdon Press/Nashville

CONTENTS

INTRODUCTION
WALKING WITH GOD

Jesus' first followers literally walked with him as he traveled throughout Galilee and Judea teaching and healing. The early Christians called their religion "the Way," suggesting that their faith was not a set of beliefs but a journey. John Wesley, the great eighteenth-century theologian and founder of Methodism, taught that salvation is not just a moment of enlightenment when we confess our love of Christ. It is a path we travel on with Jesus until we are perfected by God's grace.

The nice thing about traveling with Jesus is that he leads the way. We just follow. Following Jesus doesn't require us to have any special knowledge or training. It doesn't require us to be perfect. Jesus invites all people to walk with him. We respond to this invitation by focusing on our journey with Christ through spiritual disciplines and habits. This study, based on *The Walk* by Adam Hamilton, examines some of these practices that keep us moving on our walk with Christ.

The first five sessions in this study each look at a different spiritual discipline: worship, listening to God, service, generosity, and witness. The sixth session examines how Jesus practiced these disciplines during his final hours on the cross. Participants will find evidence of these spiritual disciplines in Scripture and the life of Christ; they will consider how these habits affect their personal relationship with God; and they will discuss the importance of engaging in these practices both individually and with a community of faith.

Sessions include a variety of discussion prompts and learning activities. Throughout the study participants are encouraged to answer questions and record their reflections in this book. Many activities also ask participants to divide into teams of three or four for discussion and roleplaying. Participants will no doubt find that they learn as much from their peers as from the information and resources provided in this book.

This study includes six sessions:

Session 1—A Living Hallelujah

Worship is our response to God. It is how we honor God, humble ourselves before God, and pledge service to God. It also is how we remember and retell our story. While individual worship is important, it is essential that we also worship as a community of faith.

Session 2—Listening and Paying Attention

When we communicate with God, we shouldn't be the only ones talking. We listen to God by paying attention to how God is at work in the natural world, through the creative expression of God's people, through our experiences, through intuition and reason, through the presence of the Holy Spirit, and especially through God's word in Scripture.

Session 3—Here I Am, Lord, Send Me

God is always at work comforting those who are suffering and providing for those who are in need. But God doesn't work alone. God invites us to join in this work and humbly serve those in our community and world.

Session 4—Where Your Treasure Is . . .

How we use our money and resources reflects our priorities. Giving generously can be painful, and even scary at first. But when we make generosity a priority and habit, we find that we are blessed as much as those who have received our gifts.

Session 5—Going Fishing, Reflecting Light

Christ calls us to be his witnesses, to spread the good news of his love and grace to the world. We act as witnesses through our words, our stories, our actions, and our example.

Session 6—The Five Practices from the Cross

Even in his darkest moment, Jesus set an example for us, his followers. He prayed, he recited Scripture, he served those in his care, he acted as a witness, and he generously gave everything, sacrificing himself for others.

Using This Resource

This study can be used in Sunday school, during evening youth fellowship gatherings, or as part of a small group or midweek Bible study. There is not a separate leader guide for this study. All instructions for leaders and participants are found in this book. The leader of the study could be an adult or one of the student participants.

Supplies

Each activity includes a list of necessary supplies. All sessions will require the following:

- Bibles
- Pens or pencils
- A whiteboard or large sheet of paper
- Markers

Session Format

All sessions include the following.

- Opening: The sessions in this study open with a short activity to help you focus on what you'll be learning and to reflect on your personal walk with Christ.
- Discussion and Learning Activities: Sessions include a variety of discussion prompts and learning activities that give participants a deeper look into the session's topic.
- Closing: At the end of each session, you and your group will have time to reflect on what you've learned and how you will respond to what you learned. Each session will conclude with a prayer.
- Altogether, the opening, activities, and closing should take about fifty minutes.

1

A LIVING HALLELUJAH

When Jesus called his first disciples, he asked them to follow him. And his first followers did exactly that. They walked with Jesus and he traveled throughout Galilee and Judea teaching, healing, and inviting more people to follow. Scripture frequently describes our relationship with Christ as a journey. We walk with Jesus along a path, or way, that God has set before us. Following Jesus means that we are always moving toward our destination of being perfected in Christ. So how do we do this?

In the opening chapter of his book *The Walk*, author Adam Hamilton looks at how we move forward on our walk with Jesus through worship. Worship is how we, as God's creations, respond and show gratitude to our creator. Worship is how we offer ourselves to God. It often involves music, prayer, reading and reflecting on Scripture, celebrating Holy Communion, and reaffirming our commitment to serve God and God's people. We worship individually through daily prayer, and we worship together when we gather in church each week. This session corresponds to the first chapter in *The Walk*, "Worship: A Living Hallelujah."

Session Activities

Opening: Where Are You Going? (10 minutes)

Supplies: pens or pencils

Could it be that just as we gave Stella this swing set as an expression of our love for her, and in the hope that she'd enjoy adventures on it, God created this amazing planet and gave it to us as an expression of his love? Was it intended for our enjoyment and adventures? How do we respond to a gift like that?

Stella's response to our gift points to what is meant to be the most basic practice in the Christian spiritual life: We say to God, "Thank you!" and "I love you." It is the essence of worship and the most basic form of prayer.

—*Adam Hamilton,* The Walk, *pp. 18–19*

As you wait for everyone to arrive and for the group to get started, write in the space below destinations that you are traveling toward. These destinations should be goals that you are working toward or hopes you have for the future.

When everyone is present and has had a chance to write, go around the room and have each person name one or more of his or her destinations.

Then ask:

- What destinations are you moving toward on your journey of faith?
- What steps have you taken in the past week toward one of your destinations? (*A step could be performing well on a school test or project, filling out an application for a job or a camp, practicing a skill, or getting a new opportunity.*)
- What obstacles or struggles have you faced on your way to one of your destinations? (*No one should feel pressure to answer this question if they are not comfortable doing so.*)

After this time of talking about your destinations, open with the prayer below or one of your own.

God of all creation, thank you for bringing us together to begin this walk together. Guide us so that we will learn from our time together and grow closer to you through the practice of worship. Open our hearts and minds to the wisdom that you have for us today. Amen.

What Is Worship? (5 minutes)

Supplies: pens or pencils

> Worship—and with it, prayer—is the first of the five spiritual practices essential to growing and maturing in our Christian walk. It was practiced throughout Scripture, lived by Jesus, and has been a foundation of the spiritual life for God's people across the millennia. God is worthy of and desires your worship. Your soul needs worship. You were created for worship.
>
> —*Adam Hamilton*, The Walk, *p. 19*

In the space below, write five words that come to mind when you hear the word *worship*.

After everyone has had a couple minutes, have each person read aloud the words he or she has written.

Discuss:

- What words came up most frequently?
- What words surprised you most?
- What do these words tell us about what worship is and why we participate in it?
- We normally associate worship with weekly church services. Based on the words we've written down, how can we worship in other times and places?

The Creature and the Eternal (15 minutes)

Supplies: paper, markers, a whiteboard or large sheet of paper

> Let's begin by defining what worship is. In her 1936 book, Worship, Catholic writer Evelyn Underhill offered this definition: "Worship,

> *in all its grades and kinds, is the response of the creature to the
> Eternal."*
>
> —*Adam Hamilton,* The Walk, *p. 19*

Each person should start with a blank sheet of paper and should draw on his or her paper a circle or oval to represent the shape of a head. Everyone then should pass his or her paper to the person on his or her right. This person should add eyes to the face. Everyone should pass the papers to the right again. Each time participants pass the papers, the people who receive the papers should add a new feature (nose, mouth, hair, a torso, arms, legs, and so forth). There are no rules about what any of these body parts should look like (or even how many there should be).

Continue until every person has added a feature to every creature. (If you have a small number of people, you may need each person to add multiple features to each creature.) When you are finished, your group should have a collection of unique creatures.

A participant should read aloud the following:

> Like these creatures we've drawn, each one of us is a unique creation. And, as human beings, we are unique from other creatures. Unlike most of God's creations, we have a choice of whether or not we will respond to our creator.

To better understand how we, as God's unique creations, respond to our creator, look at the following three Greek words that are translated as *worship* in the New Testament.

Make three columns on a whiteboard or large sheet of paper and title each column with one of the following Greek words: *proskyneo, sebomai, latreuo.*

A volunteer then should read aloud each of the following words and definitions.

- *Proskyneo* (pro-skew-NAY-oh) describes the behavior of someone who bows down and kisses the hand of someone greater. Greek speakers in the ancient world also used it describe the behavior of loyal dogs to their masters.
- *Sebomai* (SEB-oh-migh) describes approaching someone with awe and reverence. It suggests respect and possibly even fear.
- *Latreuo* (lah-TROO-oh) describes serving a master or a superior.

Under each of these three words on your whiteboard or paper, give examples that don't involve worshiping God of how people demonstrate each of these Greek terms. (For example, *proskyneo* might describe the behavior of an obsessed fan toward a favorite music group. *Sebomai* might describe someone's reaction to a severe storm.)

Once you have at least a few items in each column, discuss:

- How are these examples similar to ways in which we worship God?
- Which of these examples don't seem to correspond to how we worship God?
- What do these examples teach us about how we can, or should, worship God?

I Worship, We Worship (10 minutes)

Supplies: Bibles and pens or pencils

> *When we worship together, we lay our burdens before God, we ask for and receive his mercy, and we are filled anew with his Spirit. We hear his Word, our marching orders for life. We feast at the Table of the Lord's Supper. And then we leave renewed, inspired, and ready to serve God and serve others for another week.*
> —*Adam Hamilton,* The Walk, *p. 28*

Discuss whether your congregation uses printed hymnals and songbooks in worship, projects song lyrics and statements of faith on a screen or monitor, or uses some combination of the two.

Even if you don't use actual books in worship, there's a good chance that many of the songs you sing and the affirmations of faith you read aloud come from some sort of hymnal or worship book used by many other churches throughout the country and around the world. For example, United Methodists use the official *The United Methodist Hymnal* and *The United Methodist Book of Worship*.

If you aren't familiar with what books or worship resources your congregation uses, a member of your group should check with someone on the pastoral staff or worship team before you meet for this session. If possible, you might have someone on the pastoral staff or worship team talk with your group about how hymns, prayers, and statements of faith are selected to include in a worship service.

- Romans 12:2 says that we should not be "conformed" to this world but "transformed by the renewing" of our minds. How are we transformed in worship?
- How does worship allow us to "figure out what God's will is" (verse 2)?

Going Solo (5–10 minutes)

Supplies: Pens or pencils

> *One essential practice in the Christian walk is to participate in weekly worship with others. But corresponding to that corporate practice is the daily worship we participate in within our personal lives.*
>
> *Our daily, personal worship is composed of both our prayers and our actions. In our prayers we praise, we confess, we petition God for help, and we give thanks.*
> —*Adam Hamilton,* The Walk, *p. 31*

While worshiping with a community of faith is essential to following Jesus, personal devotion to God also is important. This involves both the time we spend in prayer and our behaviors. We'll start with prayer.

In *The Walk*, Adam Hamilton invites us to pray five times a day: once in the morning when we wake up, once at each meal (three total), and once at night before we go to sleep. Think about your day, and the opportunities you have to pray.

In the spaces below, identify at least one place and an exact time you can pray at each of these times of day. See if you can identify five total:

- In the morning
- During the day (When school is in session, this means during the school day)
- In the evening

After everyone has had a couple minutes to create a prayer plan, allow volunteers to talk about the specific times and places they wrote down. Throughout the remainder of the study, check in with one another about whether you're staying faithful to your prayer plans.

Then reflect on your behaviors. In the space below, make two lists: (1) a list of actions that you can do to grow in relationship with God and others;

and (2) a list of behaviors you should avoid. The first list could include acts of service, acts of worship, or ways to show appreciation to people in your school or community. The second should include things that you actually do or would be tempted to do; the items on this list do not necessarily have to be bad, but could instead be things that would distract you from your relationships with God and others.

Take a few minutes to write, then allow volunteers to talk about some of the items on one or both of their lists.

To Do | *Not to Do*

Closing (5–10 minutes)

Supplies: a whiteboard or large sheet of paper, markers

> *The most essential dimension of prayer and worship is captured in just two words, "Thank you."*
> —*Adam Hamilton,* The Walk, *p. 31*

In this session you've discussed the importance of worship, how we worship as a community of faith, and how we worship as individuals. As the quotation above suggests, thanks is at the heart of all worship.

Divide a whiteboard or large sheet of paper into three columns. Title one column, "I am thankful for…"; title a second, "We are thankful for…"; title a third, "The world is thankful for…" The first column could include opportunities, gifts, and relationships that you are personally thankful for. The second should include ways God has blessed your congregation and community. The third should include ways in which all of God's creation has been blessed.

Discuss:

- How can we show our thanks for these blessings?

Close your time together by discussing the following questions:

- What is one thing that you learned from today's session or think about differently as a result of today's session?
- What is one thing that you will do this week in response to what you've learned or discussed today?

Close with the prayer below or one of your own:

God, thank you for this opportunity we've had to learn from one another and from you. Open our minds and hearts this week to opportunities we have to worship you, on our own or with a community of faith. Thank you for this gift of worship as a way for us to grow in our relationship with you. Amen.

2

LISTENING AND
PAYING ATTENTION

Walking with Christ along the path that God has set for us requires us to listen for God's voice. Listening for God does not mean waiting to hear a booming voice from heaven. Rather, it requires us to constantly pay attention to all of the ways that God communicates with us. Many of the ways God speaks to us are subtle, and lots of other voices compete for our attention.

In the second chapter of his book *The Walk*, author Adam Hamilton looks at the many ways we listen for God's voice. God speaks to us through the natural world, the arts, and our personal experiences. God communicates with us in the person of the Holy Spirit, who is always present with us, guiding and comforting us. And God speaks to us more directly through the Scriptures, which is why it is important to read Scripture as a regular practice both on our own and together with others. Finally, we hear God most clearly by looking to the person of Jesus. Through his teaching and example, Jesus shows us God's will for our lives.

This session corresponds to the second chapter in *The Walk*, "Study: The Importance of Listening and Paying Attention."

Session Activities

Opening: Where Are You Going? (5–10 minutes)

Supplies: pens or pencils

To be Christians involves following Jesus' lead and listening to his voice.

—*Adam Hamilton,* The Walk, *p. 43*

As you wait for everyone to arrive and for the group to get started, list in the appropriate spaces below people whom you almost always listen to and people whom you have trouble listening to.

People I always listen to | *People I have trouble listening to*

When everyone is present and has had a chance to write, discuss:

- Why are you likely to listen to the people you listed in the first column?
- Why do you struggle to listen to the people you listed in the second column?
- What is the difference between listening and just hearing what people have to say?

Then look back on the destinations you wrote down as a part of the opening activity for the previous session (on page 9). Discuss:

- What steps have you taken in the past week toward one of your destinations?
- What obstacles or struggles have you faced on your way to one of your destinations?

After this time of talking about your destinations, open with the prayer below or one of your own.

God of all creation, thank you for bringing us back together to continue our walk. Guide us so that we will learn from our time together and grow closer to you through listening for your voice. Open our hearts and minds to the wisdom that you have for us today. Amen.

General Revelation (15–20 Minutes)

Supplies: Bibles and pens or pencils

> *General revelation . . . is often used to describe what we learn of God from observing the world that God has made, including not only nature, but the arts, our human story, and more.*
> —*Adam Hamilton,* The Walk, *p. 43*

A participant should read aloud the following:

> Listening to God isn't just about using our ears. It involves using all of our senses to pay attention to God's revelation. The word *revelation* derives from the word *reveal* and describes how God reveals God's self to us. Christians often talk of two types of revelation: special revelation and general revelation. General revelation explains how we experience God through the world around us and the people we encounter. Special revelation describes those things that we can know about God only because God takes initiative and reveals them to us. The Holy Spirit, Scripture, and the person of Jesus Christ are all special revelation.

To get a better understanding of general revelation, consider these ways that we experience God.

1. Nature

Participants should read aloud Psalm 8.

Discuss:
- What does this psalm tell us about how we see God at work in the natural world?
- What do the natural world and the cosmos tell us about God?
- What does this psalm tell us about God's relationship with us?

In the space at the top of the following page, list ways that you see or experience God in the natural world. This could include ways that you see the beauty and magnificence of what God has created or it could include ways that God uses the natural world to provide for God's people.

20

2. *The Arts*

Discuss:

- What comes to mind when you think about "the arts"?
- What do "the arts" include?

In the space below, list works of art (this may include songs, books, movies, plays, paintings, sculptures, and so forth) through which you see God at work. These may be works that are so incredible that they reveal the artist's God-given skill and creativity. Or they may be works that communicate God's message of love or grace or sacrifice.

After everyone has had a few minutes to write down examples, each person should name one of the works of art he or she wrote down and describe how he or she sees God at work in this piece of creative expression.

3. *Life and Experiences*

Volunteers should read aloud Matthew 13:3-9, 18-23.

In this Scripture Jesus uses a parable (a story or metaphor used to teach a lesson) to teach his followers something about God's kingdom.

Discuss:

- What point, do you think, is Jesus making through this parable?
- Why, do you think, did Jesus choose the images he did?

A participant should read aloud the following:

> Many of the people in Jesus' audience would have been familiar with the practice of planting and harvesting crops. They would

21

have understood what it meant for seeds to yield "thirty to one," "sixty to one," or "one hundred to one." Jesus used their real-world experiences to make a point about faith and spreading God's word.

Discuss:

- If Jesus were telling this parable today, what images do you think he might have used?

Divide into teams of three or four. Each team should come up with a current-day, real-world metaphor or example that they could use to teach one of the following points:

- God calls us to love enemies and strangers.
- Serving God requires us to be generous and make sacrifices.
- God's grace and forgiveness are available to all people, regardless of past behavior.

Take a few minutes to work then allow each team to explain its example.

4. Conscience, Intuition, and Reason *Spiritual Discipline*

Spend a moment in silence thinking about a time when you had a feeling or intuition that influenced your behavior. Maybe you were about to do something foolish or hurtful until a feeling or voice in your head convinced you not to. Perhaps you had an urge or conviction to be generous or do something for the good of others. Describe one such situation below.

After a few minutes, allow each person to talk about what he or she wrote down. Discuss:

- How might God be speaking to us through our conscience and intuition?

- Sometimes a sudden feeling or urge causes us to make a wise decision. Other times, we take our time and use reason to make important decisions. When have you taken your time to make a decision? How was God at work through this process?

Then discuss:

- Other than the four areas we explored—nature, the arts, experiences, and conscience—what are some other ways that God speaks to us through our lives and world?

Special Revelation (10 minutes)

Supplies: Bible, a whiteboard or large sheet of paper, and markers

Write in the space below words that come to mind when you think of the Holy Spirit.

After a minute or so, allow participants to say some of the words they wrote down.

Then volunteers should read aloud each of the following Scriptures:

- John 14:15-17
- Acts 1:7-8
- Acts 2:1-4

Based on these Scriptures, what words or phrases would you use to describe the Holy Spirit? Brainstorm these words and phrases as a group and list them on a whiteboard or large sheet of paper.

A participant should read aloud the following:

> As Christians we believe in God as three persons: God the Father, or Creator; God the Son, Jesus Christ; and God the Holy Spirit. The Holy Spirit is the person who is often most difficult for us to describe. Through the Spirit, God is always present in us and around us. We experience the Holy Spirit when opportunities

arise for us to serve God and others, when we feel God nudging us toward making a certain decision, or when we hear God speaking to us through worship or reading Scripture.

Write in the space below one way that you have experienced the Holy Spirit.

After a couple minutes, allow each participant to talk about his or her experience of the Spirit.

Scripture (5–10 minutes)

Supplies: pens or pencils

> *If we're serious about walking with God daily, knowing God and God's will for us, reading and studying Scripture will be a regular part of our lives.*
>
> *It is clear in reading the Gospels that Jesus not only read Scripture, he memorized it, prayed it, and lived it. As those who seek to follow him and walk with him, we should recognize that reading and studying Scripture will be an important part of our spiritual life.*
> —*Adam Hamilton,* The Walk, *p. 49*

Divide into teams of three or four. In your teams discuss the following questions:

- How frequently do you read the Bible?
- When you read the Bible, how much do you read? (*Do you read a chunk of verses? A few chapters?*)
- How do you read the Bible? For instance, do you read the Bible to learn about the history and culture of the people who wrote it? Do you read it for inspiration and guidance? Do you read it to better understand God and God's teaching? (*It's okay if you have more than one answer.*)

Below are some different ways that Christians read the Bible. Read through these individually or in your teams. Place an asterisk (*) by the ways in which you already read the Bible. Place an arrow by ways that you don't currently read the Bible but that you think would be beneficial.

Reading for Understanding

The Bible was written by people in the ancient Near East over the course of about one thousand years. Reading for understanding involves reading Scripture to better understand the history, culture, politics, and traditions of the people who wrote the Bible and to better understand God's role in their lives and story.

Reading for Formation

The Bible contains more than just history and story. Much of the Bible was written to offer instruction, guidance, and wisdom to the people who first read and heard it and to the people who would encounter it later. It includes laws, collections of wise sayings, Jesus' sayings and parables, and letters to early churches. We read these Scriptures not only to learn about the people and cultures who wrote them but also to grow spiritually by asking ourselves the following questions:

- What does this Scripture tell me about God?
- What does this Scripture tell me about people?
- What does this Scripture tell me about myself and God's will for me?

Praying the Scriptures and Lectio Divina

We talk and listen to God through prayer. We can incorporate Scripture into these conversations with God. One way to pray the Scriptures is to select a short passage from the Bible, reflect on its meaning for us, and put it in our own words in the form of a prayer.

Lectio Divina, (pronounced lexio deeveena), which literally means "divine reading," is a specific way of reading and praying Scripture. It begins with taking a short passage of Scripture—no more than a few verses—and reading it aloud several times. The first two times, you are listening for a single word, phrase, or idea that has special meaning for you. Then read the Scripture a third time, focusing on how the word, phrase, or idea you have chosen relates to you. Finally spend time in silent prayer, talking with God about the message you found in the Scripture.

Bible Study With Others

Much like worship and prayer, reading Scripture is meant to be done both individually *and* with a community of faith. In addition to reading and reflecting on the Bible on our own, we benefit from reading and studying with a Sunday school class or small group. Group study introduces us to perspectives that we may not have considered on our own. Discussions with other Christians may also challenge our assumptions or help us work through difficult questions. A small group Bible study also provides a safe place to talk about our struggles and our joys with supportive faith friends.

The Ultimate Revelation (5–10 minutes)

Supplies: pens or pencils

> When God sought to speak to the human race, to disclose who God is and who God calls us to be, he did not send a book, he sent a Person. Jesus was God's Word, God's message, wrapped in human flesh. Jesus once said to his disciple Philip, "Whoever has seen me has seen the Father" (John 14:9). All other words ever spoken or written about God are to be interpreted and understood in the light of this one word, "Jesus."
>
> *—Adam Hamilton,* The Walk, *p. 60*

In the space below, write the name of one person you know who exemplifies each of the following categories. (In other words, when you think of each category, what person immediately comes to mind?) You may answer with someone you know or with a well-known public figure.

- Musician

- Athlete

- Genius

- Comedian

- Animal Lover

Take a couple minutes to work, then allow volunteers to read aloud some of their examples.

A participant should read aloud the following:

> As Christians, we have faith that the Bible contains important truth about God and God's relationship with us. We also profess that God is always present in our world and lives in the person of the Holy Spirit. But we see God most clearly in the person of Jesus Christ.

As a group, brainstorm a list of words and phrases that describe Jesus. Set out Bibles so that participants can scan the first four books of the New Testament—Matthew, Mark, Luke, and John—to find descriptive words. List these on a whiteboard or large sheet of paper.

A participant should read aloud the following:

> Jesus is God in human form. Through Jesus, we can personally relate to and understand God. The more we learn about and relate to Jesus, the better we know God and understand God's will for us. Whenever we are unsure of what God is calling us to do, we should judge it against what we know about Jesus.

Closing (5–10 minutes)

Supplies: pens or pencils

> *If we would walk with God and become the people God wants us to be, we have to learn to pay attention and to listen.*
> —*Adam Hamilton,* The Walk, *p. 62*

In this session you've discussed different ways to listen to God and understand God's will. In the space below, list one specific way that you will pay attention to the word that God has for you. (For example, you could read a chapter a day from one of the Gospels to better know Jesus. You could spend fifteen minutes each day outside in silence, appreciating God's creation and reflecting on how God has blessed our world.)

Find a partner. (If need be, because of numbers, you can do a group of three.) Tell your partner what you wrote above. Commit to checking in with each other during the week to ensure that you are following through with your idea.

Close your time together by discussing the following questions:

- What is one thing that you learned from today's session or think about differently as a result of today's session?
- What is one thing that you will do this week in response to what you've learned or discussed today?

Close with the prayer below or one of your own:

God, thank you for this opportunity we've had to learn from one another and from you. Make us aware, in the days and weeks to come, of how we listen for your voice and seek to understand your will. Open our eyes, ears, and minds in the week ahead for your message for us. Amen.

3

HERE I AM, LORD, SEND ME

Words translated "serve," "service," or "serving" appear more than a thousand times in Scripture. The Bible is clear that loving God means serving God. The Bible is also clear that serving God and serving others go hand in hand. Every day we have countless opportunities to serve God and God's people. We just have to be ready to answer the call.

In the third chapter of *The Walk*, author Adam Hamilton reflects on how we answer God's call to serve. The prophet Micah teaches us that humbly serving God requires kindness and justice. Kindness involves showing compassion to the people we encounter in our daily lives and meeting their needs. Justice is about making things right. Doing justice means dealing with the bigger problems and structures that cause people to suffer.

This session corresponds to the third chapter in *The Walk*, "Serve: Here I Am, Lord, Send Me."

Session Activities

Opening: Where Are You Going? (5–10 minutes)

Supplies: pens or pencils

> *We are meant to serve God by doing his work and his will in this world. This is a simple but important truth: God's primary mode of working in the world is through people.*
> —*Adam Hamilton*, The Walk, *p. 67*

As you wait for everyone to arrive and for the group to get started, write in the space below ways that people have showed kindness to you in the past week.

When everyone is present and has had a chance to write, discuss:

- Which of your examples involve family and close friends?
- Which of your examples involve strangers?
- Which, if any, involve people you don't normally get along with?
- How did you respond to these acts of kindness?

Then look back on the destinations you wrote down as a part of the opening activity for the first session (on page 9). Discuss:

- What steps have you taken in the past week toward one of your destinations?
- What obstacles or struggles have you faced on your way to one of your destinations?

After this time of talking about your destinations, follow up on your ideas for paying closer attention to God's word for you. (See page 27.) Were you able to follow through on your idea? If not, why? Were you better able to hear God's word or understand God's will? What, if anything, was difficult about what you chose to do?

Then open with the prayer below or one of your own.

God of all creation, thank you for bringing us back together to continue our walk. Guide us so that we will learn from our time together and grow closer to you by reflecting on how we serve you and your people. Open our hearts and minds to the wisdom that you have for us today. Amen.

Do Justice, Love Kindness, Walk Humbly With God (10–15 minutes)

Supplies: Bibles, pens or pencils, and online dictionaries

> *Doing justice, loving kindness, practicing love—these are intertwined. Doing justice entails practicing kindness. Practicing kindness is an expression of love and justice.*
> —*Adam Hamilton,* The Walk, *p. 74*

Look up Micah 6:8 in the translation most used by your congregation or youth ministry. (It is important that everyone in the group uses the same translation.)

Write this verse in the space below.

- Take a minute to read the verse silently to yourself several times.
- Then, as a group, read aloud the verse together five times.
- Close your books. Recite the verse together without looking at it.
- Wait one full minute. Without reopening your books, recite the verse together again.
- At various points throughout this session, stop to recite Micah 6:8 to make sure that everyone still remembers it.

Ask:

- According to this verse, what does God expect from us?
- What, do you think, does the prophet Micah (the author of this verse) mean when he talks about *justice*?

Take a moment to look up *justice* in several online dictionaries. Have participants read aloud these definitions. Then write a definition in your own words in the space below.

A participant should read aloud the following:

Justice has many meanings in our language and culture, but one common theme across all these definitions is making things right.

31

Scripture teaches us that God's justice involves serving the people among us who are hurting and struggling and making sure that they are treated fairly, are able to meet their needs, and have the opportunity to live full lives.

Divide into teams of three or four. Brainstorm and list on a large sheet of paper examples of injustice, in which people are hurting, struggling, or in need. (Examples might include hunger, a certain medical condition that causes people to suffer, wars, and so forth.)

After spending a couple minutes brainstorming and discussing how injustice applies to the examples, select one of the situations you listed. Come up with ways to show kindness to people who may be affected by this instance of injustice. Then come up with ways to seek justice. For instance, if you choose hunger, you could show kindness to those affected by sharing a meal with them. Justice for hungry people would involve establishing programs and resources to make nutritional food available to anyone who needs it.

Spend two or three minutes coming up with examples. Then each team should present the situation it chose and its examples of kindness and justice.

Discuss:

- Based on what we did in this activity, what would you say is the difference between kindness and justice?
- How are kindness and justice related?

Sure, I'll Do It (15 minutes)

Supplies: Bibles and pens or pencils

> Mary said, "Here am I, the servant of the Lord; let it be with me according to your word" (Luke 1:38 NRSV). What would happen if that became our prayer every morning? How would our lives be different? How would your communities change if everyone in your church started each day on their knees, saying, "Here I am, Lord, do with me whatever you want"?
> —*Adam Hamilton*, The Walk, p. 75

Discuss:

- What is one situation where you were eager to volunteer for something?

- What is one situation where you hoped not to get chosen or called on for something?

Divide into two teams. Each team should read and answer questions about one of the assigned Scriptures.

Team 1: Isaiah 6:1-10

Read aloud Isaiah 6:1-10.

These verses are set during a time when the powerful Assyrian empire was expanding and threatening smaller nations such as Judah, where Isaiah lived. God needed a prophet to speak to God's people and guide them and give them hope during this difficult time.

Answer the following questions:

- What vision does Isaiah see?
- What does the winged creature do to Isaiah? What do you think this represents?
- What does God ask?
- How does Isaiah respond?

Team 2: Luke 1:26-38

Read aloud Luke 1:26-38.

Mary was pregnant even though she was not only a virgin but also was engaged to be married. Becoming pregnant when she was unmarried was scandalous and could have put Mary in great danger.

Answer the following questions:

- How does the angel Gabriel approach Mary?
- What does Gabriel call Mary to do?
- What questions and concerns does Mary have?
- How does Mary answer God's call?

After both teams have had about five minutes, each team should briefly summarize its Scripture and the answers to its questions.

In the space on the next page, list two or three ways that God has called you to serve. This could involve an opportunity to volunteer for a ministry at your church or participate in a service project. It could involve feeling compelled to raise awareness about a certain cause. It could involve finding yourself in a situation where you can help someone or meet someone's needs.

Allow volunteers to talk about ways God has called them to serve. Then discuss:

- What do these examples tell us about the ways that God calls us to serve?
- How have you answered God's call to serve?
- When have you missed an opportunity to answer God's call?

A volunteer should read aloud Ephesians 2:8-10.
Discuss:

- What does it mean that we are saved by God's grace rather than by something we had done?
- What does God save us from?
- According to verse 10, what does God save us for?
- How do these verses relate to God's call to serve?

Group Work (5 minutes)

Supplies: a whiteboard or large sheet of paper and markers

> *I've known people who criticize "organized religion." But when I look at organized religion, I find it to be much more impactful than disorganized religion or solitary religion.*
> —*Adam Hamilton,* The Walk, *p. 71*

Divide a whiteboard or large sheet of paper into three columns. Label one column, "Ways to show God's love." Label the second, "Individually." Label the third, "Together."

List in the first column different ways that we can show people God's love. Examples include, "healing," "hospitality," "feeding," and so forth.

For each example listed in the first column, write an example in the second column of how an individual might serve someone in that way. In the third column write a way that we, as a group or community of faith, might serve someone. For instance, an individual way to heal might be to provide a listening ear to someone who is hurting or to provide first aid to someone who has been injured. A "together" way to heal may involve building a clinic and providing medical resources to a community that doesn't have a hospital.

Discuss:

- What opportunities to serve individually are already available to you?
- What opportunities are there for you to serve as a part of a larger group?
- Look back at the chart that we made. What does the chart tell us about the importance of serving as a part of the group?
- What can we accomplish together that we would not be able to do individually?

Interrupted (10–15 minutes)

Supplies: Bibles and pens or pencils

> *Most often the opportunities to serve and show kindness are unplanned—they are interruptions. Part of what is necessary to serve Christ by serving others is our willingness to be interrupted. That sounds so easy to say, but it's hard to practice. We get so busy. We have so many things to do that haven't gotten done yet that we just don't have time for an unexpected interruption. We might not even notice the other person God has put in our path.*
> —*Adam Hamilton,* The Walk, *pp. 80–81*

Divide into teams of three or four. With your team come up with a situation in which someone is very busy. (Try to come up with a situation that everyone in your team can relate to.) One such situation could involve scrambling to finish a school project while having to spend two hours each afternoon at band practice. Another situation might involve hurrying to pack and get chores done before leaving on a trip. Describe your situation in the space below.

Then imagine a way that this situation might be interrupted by a person who could use your help. This person could be a friend or family member, a complete stranger, or even someone you don't get along with. Describe this potential interruption in the space at the top of the next page.

Prepare to act out a scene involving the situation and interruption you described. A character (or characters) should talk through a decision about whether to stop what he or she is doing to help the person who needs it.

Each team should present its scene. Then discuss:

- Which of these scenes did you relate to most?
- How do we use being busy as an excuse not to serve those who could use our help?
- When have you changed your plans to help someone? What was the result?

A participant should read aloud the following:

> *Jesus' parable of the good Samaritan teaches an important lesson about prejudice and loving all people, regardless of ethnicity. But it also has a lot to say about how we respond when people need our help.*

A participant should read aloud Luke 10:30-34.
A participant then should read aloud the following:

> *Priests and Levites were considered holy men with important responsibilities at the temple. But in this story neither the priest nor the Levite stops to help the injured man. Jesus doesn't tell us why, but he makes clear that the hero of the story is the man who stops and shows compassion. Jesus calls us to make compassion and service our top priority, even if doing so gets in the way of other responsibilities.*

Closing (5 minutes)

Supplies: pens or pencils

> *If we're serious about walking with Christ, we'll cultivate the daily practice of serving God by serving others.*
> —*Adam Hamilton,* The Walk, *p. 83*

A participant should read aloud the above quotation from *The Walk*. Discuss:

- How can we practice serving? What does that look like?

One way to practice serving is to find ways to volunteer your time and talents. Write in the space below one way that you could volunteer to serve others in the coming week.

Another way to practice serving is through prayer. Write a short prayer below asking God to make you more aware of people who could use your help and compassion. Commit to saying this prayer several times a day.

Close your time together by discussing the following questions:

- What is one thing that you learned from today's session or think about differently as a result of today's session?
- What is one thing that you will do this week in response to what you've learned or discussed today?

Close with the prayer below or one of your own:

God, thank you for this opportunity we've had to learn from one another and from you. Make us aware, in the days and weeks to come, of how we can bring kindness and justice to those who need it most. Open our eyes, ears, and minds in the week ahead for your message for us. Amen.

4

WHERE YOUR TREASURE IS . . .

Few things have had as much of an impact on human civilization as money. We are producers and consumers. We sell people products and services that they want or need so that we can buy products and services that we want or need. This is basic economics. But the Bible, which has quite a bit to say about money, teaches us that how we manage our money shouldn't be about what we want or need; it should be about what God wants and needs.

In this fourth chapter of *The Walk,* author Adam Hamilton looks at how we use the gifts that God has given us. Scripture teaches us that we should give a portion of what we have back to God. We do this by supporting the church and by being generous toward all of God's people, particularly those who are in need. Giving generously can be a struggle at first, but as we make generosity a habit, it becomes a blessing and source of happiness.

This session corresponds to the fourth chapter in *The Walk,* "Give: Where Your Treasure Is . . ."

Session Activities

Opening: Where Are You Going?

> *It struck me that [my accountant] was describing for me, in the language of economics and accounting, a lesson that Jesus taught in the Sermon on the Mount: that what we do with our money*

tells us something about the condition of our heart. Jesus said it this
way: "Where your treasure is, there your heart will be also."
—*Adam Hamilton*, The Walk, *p. 90*

As you wait for everyone to arrive and for the group to get started, think about the best and worst purchases you have ever made. Your best purchase should be something you bought that had a lasting impact and ended up being worth far more than anything you could have paid for it. Your worst purchase should be something that you knew early on was a waste of money.

Best Purchase | *Worst Purchase*

When everyone is present and has had a chance to write, allow time for volunteers to talk about their best and worst purchases.

- How do you decide, when buying something, whether what you're buying is worth the money? (*This could involve a major purchase or a small one.*)
- What, do you think, causes you to make bad decisions with your money?
- In addition to money, what other things do we have to be careful to use wisely?

Then look back on the destinations you wrote down as a part of the opening activity for the first session (on page 9). Discuss:

- What steps have you taken in the past week toward one of your destinations?
- What obstacles or struggles have you faced on your way to one of your destinations?

After this time of talking about your destinations, follow up on your ideas for paying closer attention to God's word for you. (See page 27.) Were you able to follow through on your idea? If not, why? Were you better able to hear God's word or understand God's will? What, if anything, was difficult about what you chose to do?

Then open with the following prayer or one of your own.

God of all creation, thank you for bringing us back together to continue our walk. Guide us so that we will learn from our time together and grow closer to you by reflecting on how we use our money and resources. Open our hearts and minds to the wisdom that you have for us today. Amen.

Can't Buy Happiness (10 minutes)

Supplies: Bibles, pens or pencils, a whiteboard or large sheet of paper, marker

> We live in a society where every voice around us is telling us just the opposite of Jesus' teaching—that our lives, in fact, do revolve around an abundance of stuff we own. Our culture tells us that, if we just had better, bigger, nicer, or cooler stuff, we'd be happier and more fulfilled.
>
> —*Adam Hamilton*, The Walk, *p. 91*

As a group, brainstorm a list of all the places where you encounter advertisements. Consider not only obvious ads such as social media ads, commercials, and billboards, but also any situation where a company has sponsored an event or hired someone to endorse its product. Write these on a whiteboard or large sheet of paper.

Then discuss:

- How many ads, do you think, do you see on a daily basis? (The exact number of ads a person sees varies from person to person but the number for most people likely is in the thousands.)
- What messages do you see and hear in these advertisements? In what ways are these ads trying to sell you a certain product?
- On a scale from 0 to 10 (with "0" meaning "not at all" and "10" meaning "entirely"), how much, do you think, do advertisements influence how you spend your money?

Think about one of your possessions you have that you desired the most before you got it. Name this possession in the space below, then describe what it took for you to get it. (For example, did you have to beg for it as a birthday or Christmas present? Did you save your money for weeks or months? Did you wait for months or years for a product to be released?)

Divide into teams of three or four. Talk to one another about the possessions you wrote down. Then discuss:

- How, if at all, did your life change when you got this possession you'd been wanting?
- Did the possession live up to your expectations? Why, or why not?
- How long did it take before you no longer cared about this possession or before you found yourself wanting something more, or something else entirely?

Participants should read aloud Ecclesiastes 2:4-11. *Note*: The writer of Ecclesiastes, who some translations identify as King Solomon, refers to himself as the "teacher."

Discuss:

- How does the teacher feel about all of his or her possessions and accomplishments?
- What conclusion does the teacher reach? How do these verses relate to our discussion about possessions?

Meaningful Giving (10–15 minutes)

Supplies: Bibles, pens or pencils

> *As you give thanks for what you have, you find contentment and freedom; you possess your possessions rather than your possessions possessing you.*
> —*Adam Hamilton,* The Walk, *p. 97*

Take one minute to write in the space below people and things you are thankful for.

Now take another minute. In the space below, brainstorm all of the people and things that played a part in bringing you here today. This would include anyone who gave you a ride, the car that you rode or drove in, the shoes you walked in, the building you're meeting in, and so forth.

Look over your two lists. Are there any items that appear on both lists? If so, circle these items.

Then discuss:

- Based on this activity, what are some things that you take for granted? (*In other words, what are some things that you overlook or don't give thanks for even though they're important to your life?*)
- What are some things that you are (or should be) thankful for that you wouldn't normally think to be thankful for?
- Whom do you need to say thanks to?
- How does being thankful for what you have affect decisions about how you use your money?

If we want to find fulfillment, we should look to see what is "meaning-full." What adds meaning to our lives? What gives us fulfillment and a sense of purpose every day? The Christian answer is following Jesus.

Look back on Ecclesiastes 2:4-11 (which you read as a part of the previous activity). Discuss:

- The "teacher" in Ecclesiastes says that a life focused on wealth, possessions, and accomplishments is meaningless. If this is the case, what does a meaningful life look like?

Volunteers should read aloud each of the following Scriptures. For each one, discuss:

- What do these verses have to say about finding meaning and purpose in life?

Scriptures:

- Ecclesiastes 4:4-8
- Mark 8:34-38
- 1 John 4:7-11

Based on what you discovered in these Scriptures, describe in the space below one way you can make your life more meaningful.

Take a couple minutes to work, then allow volunteers to read aloud their ideas.

A Generous Community (15–20 minutes)

Supplies: a member of your pastoral staff or finance committee or report from the church office, pens or pencils, Bibles

> *When we individually give our tithes and offerings as an expression of worship and gratitude to God, we also make it possible for the church to have a collective impact on the world around us that is vast compared to what we can achieve alone.*
> —*Adam Hamilton,* The Walk, *p. 99*

If possible arrange beforehand to have a member of your pastoral staff or someone from the church finance committee to talk to your group about ways that the church uses its money. This person should focus on money spent on congregational care, outreach, and mission. (If no one is available, see if you can get a report from the church office that shows how money is spent to help and care for others.)

Discuss:

- How does our church get money?
- What sorts of expenses does our church have?

Listen as one of your church leaders goes over how money is spent or look over the report from the church office. If someone is able to talk with your group, allow time for questions. Then discuss:

- What, if anything, surprised you about how the church spends its money?
- What sorts of things are we able to do as a congregation that one person wouldn't be able to do alone?

Participants then should read aloud each of the following Scriptures. For each one, discuss:

- What does this Scripture say about giving our money and resources to God and the church?

Scriptures:

- Leviticus 27:30-34
- Deuteronomy 15:7-8
- Luke 21:1-4
- 2 Corinthians 9:7

Cheerful Givers

Supplies: Bibles

> *When we are generous, we find joy. And just as we were made to practice generosity together, in community, God also means for it to be a part of the daily rhythm of our lives.*
> —*Adam Hamilton,* The Walk, *p. 101*

A participant should read aloud 2 Corinthians 9:7 again. Discuss:

- What, do you think, does Paul (the author of this verse) mean by a "cheerful giver"?

Divide into teams of three or four. Each team should act out two scenes involving someone who has an opportunity to give of his or her money (or possessions or time). The first scene should show someone who does not give cheerfully. The second scene should show someone who is a cheerful giver.

After teams have had a few minutes to prepare, each team should present both of its scenes.

Then discuss:

- Why does our attitude matter when we give of our money and resources?
- For what reasons might we be reluctant to give or have a negative attitude about giving?
- How might our attitude about giving change the more that we do it?

A participant should read aloud:

> *God loves cheerful givers. The good news is that generosity makes us cheerful. At first, giving is difficult. We don't want to let go of money that we've earned, and we don't want to sacrifice our plans to help other people. But as giving becomes habit, it becomes less of a burden. It's just part of who we are and what we do. When generosity is our way of life, it brings us joy and often inspires us to be even more generous.*

Closing (5–10 minutes)

Supplies: pens or pencils

> *When we practice generosity over and over, it becomes part of the rhythm of our lives, our hearts become attuned to God's desire for us, and we come to walk more closely with him.*
> —Adam Hamilton, The Walk, *p. 109*

Write in the space below things that you could give generously. Do not limit your list to money or even possessions. Consider your abilities and talents also.

Then write in the space below specific ways you can give of things you listed above. As you write, reflect on how you could follow through on these ideas.

Close your time together by discussing the following questions:

- What is one thing that you learned from today's session or think about differently as a result of today's session?
- What is one thing that you will do this week in response to what you've learned or discussed today?

Close with the prayer below or one of your own:

God, thank you for this opportunity we've had to learn from one another and from you. Make us aware, in the days and weeks to come, of how we can practice generosity. Use these actions to shape our hearts, make us more generous, and help us live according to your will. Open our eyes, ears, and minds to you in the week ahead. Amen.

5

GOING FISHING, REFLECTING LIGHT

Jesus calls us to be his witnesses and to spread the good news of Christ's love wherever we go. This means telling our faith story and letting people know that we are followers of Christ, both through our words and through our actions. This can be challenging. Even if we are confident in our faith, talking about it or drawing attention to it can be uncomfortable. We don't want people to think we're being pushy or judgmental, and we often have trouble talking about things that are personal. But if we work through these challenges, the Holy Spirit will work through us to bring the love and message of Christ to everyone we interact with.

In the fifth chapter of *The Walk*, Adam Hamilton looks at how we can make a habit of being witnesses. Witnessing involves telling our faith story— the story of how we came to be in a relationship with Jesus. We do this by our words, but we also do this by our actions and example, letting the light of Christ shine through us. And like other practices, such as worship and service, witnessing is something that we do both individually and as a community of faith.

This session corresponds to the fifth chapter in *The Walk*, "Share: Going Fishing, Reflecting Light."

Session Activities

Opening (10 minutes)

Supplies: pens or pencils

As everyone arrives, come up with an amazing story about yourself. This story may be true or false. BUT if the story is true, you want it to be so incredible that people might think it's false. (So don't tell a story that a lot of people in the group would know.) If the story is false, you want people to think that it might be true.

When most everyone is present, have each person tell his or her story. After each story, participants should vote on whether they think the story is true or false. Award a point to the creator of each story for each person he or she fools. When everyone has gone, declare a winner.

Then look back on the destinations you wrote down as a part of the opening activity for the first session (on page 9). Discuss:

- What steps have you taken in the past week toward one of your destinations?
- What obstacles or struggles have you faced on your way to one of your destinations?

Then open with the prayer below or one of your own.

God of our lives and our stories, thank you for bringing us back together to continue our walk. Guide us so that we will learn from our time together and grow closer to you by reflecting on how we bear witness to your love and your story. Open our hearts and minds to the wisdom that you have for us today. Amen.

Can I Get a Witness? (5 minutes)

> *As we talk about our faith, our experiences of God's love, of Christ's presence in our lives, of being a part of a church, of new insights into faith, or of the impact our faith has on our lives, we find our faith in Christ actually deepens and becomes more real to us. It is in giving away our faith, sharing it with others, that our faith and our spiritual passion grow.*
>
> —*Adam Hamilton,* The Walk, *p. 114*

Discuss:

- What comes to mind when you hear the word *witness*?
- In what situations would someone be a witness?

You probably hear the word *witness* most often in reference to court cases. Discuss:

- Based on what you know from school or from books, movies, and television, what do you know about the role of a witness in a trial?
- What makes a witness in a court case effective?

A participant should read aloud the following:

> Witnesses in a trial give testimony, which is their honest description of what they saw or experienced. Jesus calls us to be his witnesses. This means telling the world about our experience of Jesus.

Discuss:

- How do you feel about being a witness for Jesus? What is intimidating about telling your story? What is exciting about it?

Elevator Speeches (10 minutes)

Supplies: A whiteboard or large sheet of paper, markers, and pens or pencils

> Most people who choose to follow Jesus do so because of the positive witness of Christians *through whom they experienced love and from whom they heard a compelling witness and example of what it means to be a Christian. In other words, most people who become Christians do so because of the "positive reviews" of others who have become Christians.*
> —*Adam Hamilton,* The Walk, *p. 118*

As a group, brainstorm the truths about Jesus that are most important for people to know. Write these on a whiteboard or large sheet of paper.

An "elevator speech" is a talk that is meant to get someone really excited about something in a very short period of time. (For example, if you were a screenwriter and you ended up sharing an elevator with a big-time movie producer, what would you say to this person on your short elevator ride to get him or her excited about your idea?)

Come up with an elevator speech to get people excited about Jesus. You can draw from the list you just made as a group, and you can draw from your personal experience. But your speech should last no more than thirty seconds. (As needed, record notes in the space below.)

After everyone has had a couple minutes to work, divide your group into pairs. Each pair should select a Person A and Person B. Set a timer for thirty seconds and have Person A give his or her elevator speech to Person B. Then switch places and set the timer again. This time Person B should give his or her speech to Person A. (If you have an odd number of people, you may have a group of three or have an adult leader pair with one participant.)

Discuss:

- What did you learn about Jesus, or having a relationship with Jesus, from your partner's speech?
- What did you learn about your partner from their speech?
- Why is it good to be able to have a thirty-second description of your faith and relationship with Christ?
- What are the shortcomings of telling your faith story in only thirty seconds?
- What if you had to describe your faith in a single sentence? What would the sentence be?

You—Plural—Are My Witnesses (5 minutes)

Supplies: Bibles and pens or pencils

> *What leads the unchurched to take notice of a church is when that church and its members genuinely care about them and when the church is actively engaged in seeking to have a positive impact on the community. They notice when a church serves others selflessly, when it gives generously, when it is loves radically.*

This is what Jesus had in mind, I think, when he told his disciples, "Let your light shine before people, so they can see the good things you do and praise your Father who is in heaven."
—*Adam Hamilton,* The Walk, *p. 127*

Discuss:

- In English, what is the second-person singular pronoun?
- In English, what is the second-person plural pronoun?

A participant should read aloud:

In English, we use the word you *whether we're referring to one person or multiple people. This can make translations from other languages misleading or difficult to understand.*

A participant should read aloud Matthew 5:14-16. Discuss:

- Have you thought of *you* and *your* in this passage as referring to a single person, or a group of people? (The Greek verbs are plural, indicating a group of people.) How does the meaning of this Scripture change once you know *your* is plural?

Think about our congregation. How do we shine our light in this community? Imagine that you live in this community but that you have never been a part of this congregation and know little about it. Where might you notice this church? Where might you see it at work? Come up with a scenario where you are a member of the community who comes in contact with our congregation. Describe this situation in one or two sentences in the space below. (For example, "I saw people from _____ Church selling corn fritters at a booth at the Fall Festival." Or, "I worked with a group from _____ Church while volunteering at the downtown food bank. Or, "I visited _____ Church with a friend once, and very few people talked to me.")

Allow a couple minutes for everyone to work and then have everyone read aloud their scenario.

51

Discuss:

- What does this activity teach us about how our congregation is at work in the community and how people see us?
- How does our congregation act as a witness for Jesus Christ?

A participant should read aloud the following.

> In previous sessions we saw that practices such as worship, service, and generosity have a personal dimension and a community dimension. The same is true for witnessing. We have a personal story to tell, but we also tell a story as a community of faith. When we do mission and outreach work, when we do fun activities as a group, and when people visit our congregation or participate in its ministries, we are witnesses. People learn about Jesus through us. We have a responsibility to be faithful with our witness.

Discuss:

- What can we do, as a church or as a youth ministry, to be faithful witnesses of Christ?

Gentleness and Respect (10 minutes)

Supplies: thank-you notes or notebook paper, pens or pencils (Stamps or envelopes are optional.)

> *If you are a Christian it is because faith was shared with you by someone.*
> —Adam Hamilton, The Walk, *p. 120*

Divide into teams of four or five. In your teams, everyone should imagine that he or she is not a Christian and is not very familiar with Christianity and the church. Discuss:

- What things that Christians do and talk about would make you interested in becoming a Christian and joining the church? Why?
- What things that Christians do and talk about would push you away from the Christian faith? Why?
- What could you do, or do differently, to be a more effective witness?

Then take a moment to reflect on the witnesses who have had an impact on your faith. What people, through their stories or examples, brought you to faith, helped you grow in faith, or convinced you to be a part of the church?

Select one of these persons and write a thank-you note or letter, telling them about the influence they had on your faith and thanking them for their witness. If possible, send or deliver your letter to this person.

Practicing Our Witness (10–15 minutes)

Supplies: Bibles

> *None of us are perfect in how we live out our faith. But we are all called by Jesus to live and share our faith in such a way that others see him in us. The apostle Paul described himself and his colleagues as "Christ's ambassadors," and he believed that God was making his appeal to others through them. Jesus told his disciples to go into all the world and make disciples, teaching the things he had taught and baptizing others who would accept his call.*
> —Adam Hamilton, *The Walk, p. 117–118*

A participant should read aloud Acts 1:6-8. Discuss:

- What does Jesus command his followers to do in these verses?

A participant should read aloud the following:

> *Jesus calls us to be his witnesses. Like any other spiritual discipline, witnessing requires practice. We need to seek opportunities to tell our faith story and invite people into a relationship with Jesus.*

As a group come up with a scenario in which one person has an opportunity to be a witness to the other. Have pairs of volunteers role-play this situation, with one person playing the role of the witness and one playing the role of the person being witnessed to. The person witnessing should focus on being honest, positive, and nonjudgmental. The person being witnessed to should respond honestly, even if that means asking tough questions.

Have each pair role-play the situation for about a minute.

Then discuss:

- What opportunities do you have to be a witness for Christ?
- What tough questions might you face as a witness for Christ?
- Which of these questions do you not have an answer for?

A participant should read aloud:

> As Christ's witnesses, we should be prepared to tell people about our relationship and experience with Jesus. We won't always have the answers to every question. What's important is that we are honest and sincere.

Closing (5 minutes)

Supplies: pens or pencils

> *Go back and take another look at... the people who helped you to know Christ or to deepen your faith. I'd encourage you to stop and thank God for them. And then to ask God to use you, that your name might appear on someone else's list years from now, as the person who shared your faith.*
> —*Adam Hamilton,* The Walk, *p. 136*

This session has focused mostly on *how* we are Christ's witnesses. But it is also important to know why.
Discuss:

- Why, do you think, is it important to be witnesses for Christ?
- How has God worked through you or someone you know to bring someone into a relationship with Christ?

A participant should read aloud the following.

> While we have a role to play in spreading Christ's message, the Holy Spirit does the actual work of bringing someone into a relationship with Christ. When we share our witness, we are in a partnership with God.

Close your time together by discussing the following questions:

- What is one thing that you learned from today's session or think about differently as a result of today's session?

- What is one thing that you will do this week in response to what you've learned or discussed today?

Close with the prayer below or one of your own:

God, thank you for this opportunity we've had to learn from one another and from you. Give us the wisdom and courage to be your witnesses through our words, actions, and example. Open our eyes, ears, and minds in the week ahead for your message for us. Amen.

6

THE FIVE PRACTICES FROM THE CROSS

Over the course of this study we've examined a variety of spiritual practices: worship, listening to God, service, generosity, and witness. These practices enrich our lives and draw us into a closer relationship with Christ. The Gospels show us that all of these practices were a part of Jesus' life and ministry, and he was faithful to these habits even during his final hours on the cross.

In the sixth and final chapter of *The Walk*, author Adam Hamilton considers Jesus' time on the cross. Even as Jesus was dying, he prayed, he quoted Scripture, he served others, he gave generously of himself, and he was a witness of God's redeeming love. In his death, Jesus made the ultimate sacrifice for our redemption. Up until the end, he set a perfect example of how to live a faithful life.

This session corresponds to the sixth chapter in *The Walk,* "The Five Practices from the Cross."

Session Activities

Opening (5–10 minutes)

Supplies: pens or pencils

> *Jesus spoke seven different times [from the cross]...*

As we turn to these statements, we'll see evidence that, even from the cross, Jesus was pursuing the five essential practices.
　　　　　　　—*Adam Hamilton,* The Walk, *p. 142–143*

As participants arrive, see how much you remember about the topics and spiritual practices you've learned about and discussed over the course of this study. In the space below, list as many of these topics and practices as you can remember.

When most participants are present, a volunteer should read aloud his or her list. Other participants should place a check mark by any item that also is on their lists. Another volunteer should read aloud any items on his or her list that the first person didn't name. Continue until no one has any additional items to read.

A participant should read aloud the following.

> This study has focused on spiritual practices that move us along our journey of faith and draw us closer to God. This session will look at how Jesus practiced several of these practices from the cross.

Then look back on the destinations you wrote down as a part of the opening activity for the first session (on page 9). Discuss:

- What steps have you taken in the past week toward one of your destinations?
- What obstacles or struggles have you faced on your way to one of your destinations?

Then open with the prayer below or one of your own.

God of our lives and our stories, thank you for bringing us back together to continue our walk. Guide us so that we will learn from our time together and grow closer to you by reflecting on all of the spiritual habits we've learned about during this study. Open our hearts and minds to the wisdom that you have for us today. Amen.

Prayers From the Cross (10 minutes)

Supplies: Bibles

> It should not surprise us that three of the last seven statements
> Jesus makes before his death are prayers.... The Gospels record that
> Jesus prayed frequently. Prayer was a part of the daily rhythm of
> Jesus' life.
>
> —*Adam Hamilton,* The Walk, *p. 143*

Discuss:

- Imagine that you are in a situation where you are in great pain or your
  life is threatened. What would you pray in that situation?

A participant should read aloud the following:

> The second session in this study examined prayer and listening to
> God. Jesus, when he was on the cross, prayed to God.

A participant should read aloud Matthew 27:45-46.

- What is Jesus' prayer from the cross?
- This prayer is a verse from a psalm in the Old Testament. Why, do you
  think, does Jesus choose this verse?
- What, if anything, surprises you about Jesus' choice of prayer?

Skim through Psalm 22, the psalm that Jesus references on the cross. This
psalm begins with the verse that Jesus quotes in Matthew 27:46, but it says
much more. Discuss:

- The author of this psalm begins by crying out in despair. What does
  the author say about why he is in despair (see verses 6-7)?
- How does the author's tone change later in the psalm?
- What, would you say, is the main idea of this psalm?

A participant should read aloud the following:

> Rather than just being a cry of despair, Jesus may have been
> referring to all of Psalm 22. In Jesus' day the Bible didn't have
> chapter and verse numbers. People often referred to the psalms
> by their opening line. By crying out the first line of Psalm 22,

Jesus referenced this entire psalm, which tells of finding hope and strength in God during a trying time.

Discuss:

- Why, do you think, did Jesus choose this psalm when he was dying on the cross?
- How does it help you to know that Jesus felt despair and anguish on the cross?
- What does it say that even in such a dark moment, Jesus chose to pray?

Scripture From the Cross (15 minutes)

Supplies: Bibles and pens or pencils

> *As you study Scripture, you will find that you are, like Jesus, able to draw upon what you've studied in Scripture to guide, shape, direct and comfort you.*
> —*Adam Hamilton,* The Walk, *p. 148*

What Bible verses do you know off the top of your head? Write some of these in the space below. These don't need to be verses that you know by heart. They can be Scripture citations (such as John 3:16) that you've seen referenced on T-shirts, church signs, or celebrity tattoos. (Even if you aren't entirely sure of the chapter and verse, write anything that you know about the verse. For instance, "something from Philippians," "something about faith, hope, and love.")

Discuss:

- Are there Bible verses that you remember and refer to during difficult times?
- If so, what makes these verses memorable? How do they give you strength and comfort?

A participant should read aloud Luke 23:44-46. Jesus' final words from the cross are from Psalm 31:5, a familiar Bible verse.

Jesus often referred to writings from the Jewish Scriptures, books that now make up our Old Testament. Look up and read the Scriptures below from the Gospel of Matthew. For each one, identify the Old Testament verse that Jesus is quoting and why he is quoting it.

You may be able to find this information in the footnotes or study notes of the Bible you're using. If not, you should be able to find this information by searching online (or by finding a study Bible in your church you can use). You can do this activity individually, in teams, or as an entire group.

Scripture	*Old Testament Verse*	*Why Jesus Quotes It*

- Matthew 4:1-4
- Matthew 5:21-24
- Matthew 19:16-22
- Matthew 22:24-30

Discuss:

- How did Jesus use Scripture in his teaching?
- What do these verses say about Jesus' familiarity with Scripture?
- How can you become more familiar with Scripture so that you can draw from it and refer to it when you need to?

Service From the Cross (10 minutes)

Supplies: Bibles and pens or pencils

> *We offer ourselves to God every day—asking God to use us, paying attention to see where others need our help, and then seeking to serve them through acts of justice, mercy, and kindness.*
> —*Adam Hamilton, The Walk, p. 149*

Write in the space below about someone who has made a sacrifice for you. This could involve a family member giving up their time to drive you to practices or scouting events; it could involve a friend allowing you to borrow something when you were in a bind; it could involve a teacher or coach investing their own money in their students' or players' success.

After a few minutes, allow volunteers to talk about the sacrifice they discussed.

Discuss:

- What motivates people to make sacrifices for others?
- What sacrifice did Jesus make?
- Why did he make this sacrifice?

A participant should read aloud John 19:25-27. Note: The "disciple whom Jesus loved" is mentioned throughout the Gospel of John but never by name. This disciple is traditionally believed to be John, who also is never mentioned by name in this Gospel.

Discuss:

- What does Jesus do during these verses?
- Jesus does this while he is on the cross, making the ultimate sacrifice. What does this tell us about Jesus' heart and priorities?
- How can you seek to better serve those closest to you, like your family?

Witnesses From the Cross (10 minutes)

Supplies: Bibles, a whiteboard or large sheet of paper, and markers

> *He wanted sinners and broken people to know that God is the God of the second chance—rich in mercy, forgiving of even the worst things we could do. And so, he regularly associated with sinners*

61

and tax collectors and prostitutes, even though the religious leaders constantly criticized him for it. He came to tell them that God is like a shepherd who cares so much about each individual sheep that he will leave the ninety-nine who are safe to go rescue one that is lost. God is like the father who joyfully celebrates the return of his prodigal son who has squandered his inheritance and messed up his life; he wraps his arms around him and throws a party, saying, "My son who is dead is alive again." That's who Jesus showed us that God is.

—*Adam Hamilton,* The Walk, *p. 154–155*

One of the most common and popular types of stories told in our culture—in books, in movies, on television, and so on—is the redemption story. These stories involve someone with a dark past changing his or her ways and becoming good.

Brainstorm a list of redemption stories you're familiar with and write them on a whiteboard or large sheet of paper. For each one, note who is redeemed and what led to their redemption.

After you have a pretty good list, discuss:

- Which of the bad people in these redemption stories were redeemed because of the words or actions of other people?
- Which of these people were redeemed late in their lives or toward the end of their story?

A participant should read aloud the following:

Christ, through his death and resurrection, atones for our sins and delivers us from death. This is God's grace. We find redemption by accepting this grace. Often, God works through other people to draw us into a relationship. These other people are witnesses.

A participant should read aloud Luke 23:32-34, 39-43.
Discuss:

- Who finds redemption in these verses?
- Who in these verses is a witness?

A participant should read aloud the following:

Even on the cross, Jesus was a witness. He sought forgiveness for all the people who were responsible for him being on the cross. This included the people directly responsible for putting him there, as well as all the people throughout history whose sins Jesus died for. The criminal next to Jesus found redemption, even in the final moments of his life. He, too, was a witness from the cross, proclaiming Jesus' innocence and asking Jesus to remember him.

Generosity from the Cross (5–10 minutes)

Supplies: Bibles and pens or pencils

> *The cross is the highest expression of generosity and self-giving. Jesus gave everything, the source of living water became thirsty, so that we might have life.*
> —*Adam Hamilton,* The Walk, *p. 153*

Think of something that you worked so hard on for so long that, when you finished, you were relieved and in the mood to celebrate. Write about this experience in the space below.

After everyone has had a few minutes to write, allow volunteers to talk about what they wrote.

Then a participant should read aloud John 19:28-30. Discuss:

• What has Jesus finished, or completed?

A participant should read aloud the following:

> When Jesus said these words from the cross, he wasn't just saying that his life was over. Rather, he was saying that he had accomplished his mission. He had given everything he could for the redemption of the world and was ready to return to his Father. Jesus kept giving of himself until his giving was complete.

Discuss:

- What can we learn from Jesus' example—especially in these verses—about generosity?

Closing (5 minutes)

It is precisely because of that divine love that we long to walk with Jesus and invite Jesus to walk with us....

The cross of Christ displays a "love so amazing, so divine," that it demands our soul, our life, our all. It calls us to love God with all that we are and to love our neighbor as we love ourselves. The five essential practices we've studied in this book are each means of growing in our love of God and others as we seek to walk with Jesus in our daily life.

—*Adam Hamilton,* The Walk, *p. 159*

Over the course of this study, we've looked at a variety of practices that move us forward on our walk with Christ.

Discuss:

- Are there any spiritual practices that you've tried or made a habit of over the course of this study? If so, what did you do and what effect did it have on your life and your faith?
- How can you make the spiritual practices that we've learned about a part of your life in the coming weeks and months? What changes do you need to make to work these practices into your life?

Close your time together by discussing the following questions:

- What is one thing that you learned from today's session or think about differently as a result of today's session?
- What is one thing that you will do this week in response to what you've learned or discussed today?

Close with the prayer below or one of your own:

God, thank you for this opportunity we've had to learn from one another and from you. Give us the wisdom and courage to be your witnesses through our words, actions, and example. Open our eyes, ears, and minds in the week ahead for your message for us. Amen.